There are still figureheads to be rediscovered. This fine lady (possibly the goddess Ceres) was found during the rebuilding of the South Shields branch of the British Legion, who presented her to the Tyne and Wear County Museum Service for restoration and display.

SHIPS' FIGUREHEADS

M. K. Stammers

Shire Publications Ltd

CONTENTS

Set in 9 on 9 point Times and printed in Great Britain by C. I. Thomas and Sons (Haverfordwest) Ltd, Press Buildings, Merlins Bridge, Haverfordwest, Dyfed.

ACKNOWLEDGEMENTS

The author acknowledges with thanks the help given by his wife, by colleagues at Merseyside County Museums, by all those with whom he has corresponded on the subject of figureheads, and by those who have provided photographs. Illustrations are acknowledged as follows: Bristol City Museum and Art Gallery, page 19 (lower); R. Jones, Merseyside Tourist Development Office, page 17; Cadbury Lamb, pages 11, 13 (top two), 16, 28 (top right), 29 (left) and cover; R. Malster, page 2; Merseyside County Museums, pages 5, 7, 8 (both), 9 (all), 10, 12 (left), 13 (lower), 14 (lower), 15 (from Mersey Docks and Harbour Board Collection), 18 (both), 19 (top two), 20 (both), 21 (both), 22 (top), 25 (both), 26, 28 (lower), 29 (right), 30 (both); Mark R. Myers and North Devon Maritime Museum, pages 14 (top left), 22 (bottom), 24 (top); National Maritime Museum, page 3; New Brunswick Museum, page 27 (both); D. Smith, page 22 (centre); Mrs T. M. Stammers, pages 14 (top right), 28 (left); Tay Division RNR, HMS *Camperdown*, Dundee, page 12 (right); Town Docks Museum, Kingston upon Hull, page 23; Tyne and Wear County Council Museum Service, page 1; J. Whitehead, page 31.

COVER: *Lord Nelson, the most famous of all naval heroes, once adorned the bows of HMS 'Trafalgar' and is now on view at HMS 'Nelson', Portsmouth.*

LEFT: *Shipwreck was frequent among merchant sailing ships and many figureheads have survived because they were rescued as souvenirs of shipwrecks. This picture shows a collection on the gable of the hut of the Lowestoft Old Company of Beachmen. The Beachmen were responsible for much salvage and rescue work off the East Anglian coast in the nineteenth century.*

The Valhalla Museum at Tresco in the Isles of Scilly has one of the finest collections of figureheads in Great Britain.

INTRODUCTION

Figureheads are an evocative reminder of the vanished age of sailing ships. Many have survived, severed from the vessels that they once adorned, souvenirs of a time when ships were a source of pride as well as profit. Large numbers of them have been cherished as trophies from shipwrecks or the scrapyard and are now displayed in museums and public places. There is a huge range of styles and standards of execution, ranging from the naive chip carving of a seaman who loved his ship to the sophisticated artist creating a baroque invocation to the power and prestige of the Royal Navy. Even today

there are still a few carvers working in the old maritime traditions, fulfilling the needs of the restorers of historic ships and the builders of new vessels for sail training.

This survey concentrates on the history of British figureheads, and mainly those of the eighteenth and nineteenth centuries, for it is only from these centuries that they have survived in large numbers. It also emphasises the typical rather than the unique, but many of the illustrations show little known figureheads. A list of the major collections is to be found at the end of the book.

RIGHT: *Some changes in figureheads from the Viking era to the thirteenth century: (from the top) figurehead of AD 400 (in British Museum) and Viking ship of the tenth century; Bayeux tapestry ship, eleventh century; thirteenth-century ship, the development of the forecastle eliminates the figurehead.*

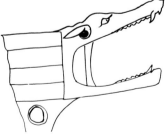

LEFT: *This wolf figurehead appears in a drawing by Holbein of a carrack of 1532.*

4

Henry VIII's carracks of 1520.

THE FIRST FIGUREHEADS

A figurehead is a carved or painted figure or emblem ornamenting the bows of a ship. Often it relates to the ship's name or its purpose. The origins of the figurehead probably lie in the earliest days of seafaring, when its purpose was religious as well as decorative. For early seafarers the figurehead was literally the head of an animal sacrificed to the sea gods to ensure a fair passage. Eventually a symbolic head was substituted for that of the victim. As well as being a propitiation of the gods, a figurehead embodied the spirit of the ship itself. It also provided a means of identification.

The seafarers of all the early Mediterranean civilisations fitted their ships with figureheads. The ships of the ancient Egyptians carried figures of holy birds and also had eyes painted on each side of the bow by which the ship could see her way across the waters. The Phoenicians favoured carvings of horses' heads, signifying speed, while the Greek rowing galleys were often fitted with bronze animals. A favourite was the boar's head, for the Greeks wanted their warship to resemble the most feared of all the animals they hunted on land. Ancient ship decoration, as with later ships, was not confined to the bows. For example, many Roman merchant vessels carried a graceful swan figure at the stern.

The Viking longships often carried serpents and dragons as extensions to their long curving stems. Some of their figureheads have survived, including two on display in the British Museum in London. The Bayeux Tapestry, showing William of Normandy's invasion fleet of 1066, depicts ships with lion and dragon figureheads. These vessels were single-masted, clinker-built, and of similar design to the earlier Viking vessels.

In the following three centuries ships continued to develop in a similar fashion. Pictures of ships of the period are scarce but are found on the seals of medieval seaports, in church carvings and in illuminated manuscripts. All these sources suggest that figureheads were popular. For naval warfare, fighting platforms were added at the bows and stern of ships. These 'castles' gradually changed from temporary structures to fully integrated parts of the hull. They concealed the stem head and the stern post and so decoration was confined to carved and painted heraldic designs around the sides of the forecastle.

Towards the end of the fourteenth century and the beginning of the fifteenth much larger, two-masted and later three-masted ships were developed. These were known as *carracks* and the carrack design appears to have revived the use of the figurehead. For example, the earliest surviving ship model, which dates from 1450 and is now in the Prins Hendrik Museum at Rotterdam, has a small animal figurehead. The carrack's forecastle was gradually extended over the bow to provide access for the crew to the bowsprit and its sail. The bowsprit was introduced as an extra spar projecting over the bow and pictures show small carved animal figureheads, often with open jaws, mounted below this spar. The carrack was the forerunner of all later deep-sea square-rigged sailing ships and was capable of long voyages across the Atlantic to the New World and beyond.

The hull and rig were enlarged and refined in the sixteenth century. By the latter half of the century the English galleons, as they were termed, were longer, with a lower superstructure and capable of carrying a bigger armament than the carrack. These ships were the basis of England's rise as a maritime power. At the bow they were built with a long low projecting structure known as the beakhead. Apart from its functional role, this provided another space for decoration. But the style of decoration owed much to the past, consisting of a small figurehead, usually an animal's head, and a mass of geometric and heraldic paintwork in bright colours extending from the beakhead along the upper part of the hull to the stern. In the next century there was a transformation in ship decoration.

The bows of the modern replica of Sir Francis Drake's ship, the 'Golden Hind', provide a good idea of the shape of the beakhead, the dominating geometric decoration and the relatively small size of the figurehead on a late sixteenth-century galleon.

The 'Sovereign of the Seas' was built for Charles I more as a symbol of naval power than as a fighting warship. Her scheme of decoration was probably the most elaborate ever carved for a British warship. Her seaworthiness was much improved by the Cromwellian navy by reducing her high upper decks. She remained in the Royal Navy until 1696. She was fitted with the low beakhead. This was changed in warships of the later seventeenth century.

NAVAL FIGUREHEADS

In the seventeenth century there was a great increase in naval activity as the nations of Europe competed for trade and empires. Britain, France, Holland and the Scandinavian countries were all building up their navies. The new warships were substantially bigger than their predecessors and set a pattern for battleship design which continued into the following century. They were three-masted vessels which carried their main armament usually on two or three decks, with upwards of one hundred muzzle-loading cannon.

Styles of ship decoration changed radically as well. The galleons of Elizabethan England had been decorated with heraldic and geometric devices and perhaps a small figure on their beakhead, a development of the medieval tradition, while the seventeenth-century warships were highly decorated in an elaborate baroque style which must have derived from the artistic and architectural styles ashore. The figurehead formed part of a larger overall scheme of decoration and was supported by a multiplicity of allegorical figures, caryatids, putti and other devices borrowed from classical architecture. Decoration ran round the whole length of the ship from the figurehead and its supporting timbers along the sides, with carved wreaths round the upper gunports, to the richly carved stern. Much of the carving was gilded and the appearance of the vessel was intended to reflect the power and prestige of the nation or its monarch.

An early peak in this style was the *Sovereign of the Seas*. She was built in

ABOVE: *The lion, symbolising aggression and power, became the most popular warship figurehead in the seventeenth century. Often he was shown crowned and leaping forward from the bows of the ship. The other main components of the bow structure were also elaborately carved and the carvings were continued along the upper part of the hull to an equally elaborate stern. This is the Navy Board model of the ninety-gun ship HMS 'Neptune' of 1683.*

1637 on the orders of Charles I and was intended to be the biggest and finest warship afloat. She had an elaborately decorated beakhead with the knightly figure of King Edgar, an Anglo-Saxon king, on horseback conquering seven provincial kings; behind these figures was a wealth of carved heraldic beasts and devices. These were continued along the upper deck back to the stern. All the carved work was gilded and the bill for decoration amounted to nearly £7000 out of the total building cost of £40,000. Her Dutch enemies nicknamed her the 'Golden Devil'.

The *Sovereign of the Seas* retained the low forward-projecting beakhead which had developed in the galleons of the previous century. But in later warships this forward projection was increased in height and the figurehead itself was gradually placed in a more vertical position. This helped to make the vessel more seaworthy, for the position of the low beakhead allowed it to scoop up seas, causing damage to the elaborate carvings.

Information about figureheads becomes more plentiful in the seventeenth century, and several figureheads are preserved. The most spectacular of these

BELOW: *The lion was the dominant figurehead not only for the British navy but for most other navies of the late seventeenth and early eighteenth centuries. This fact was recognised in one of the first textbooks on naval architecture, Sutherland's 'Shipbuilder's Assistant' of 1711.*

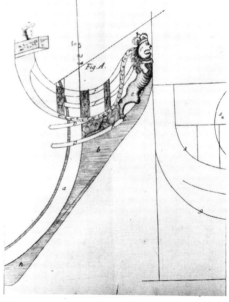

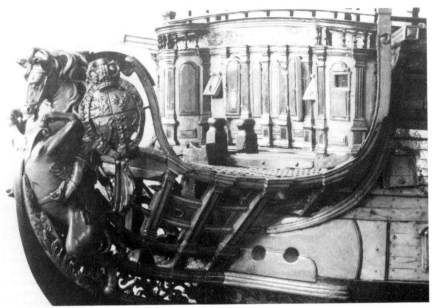

ABOVE: *Although the lion was almost the standard figurehead for the Royal Navy for the first three decades of the eighteenth century, first-rate warships (of over a hundred guns) were permitted very elaborate decoration, as this Navy Board model of the 'St George' of 1714 shows.*
BELOW: *The stern of an early eighteenth-century first-rate ship was probably even more highly decorated than the bows, with a riot of allegorical figures running over the stern galleries. This is the after end of the 'St George' model.*

By the mid eighteenth century the human figure was displacing the lion as the most popular emblem for the smaller naval vessels. Many were positioned with their legs astride the stem, almost kneeling, a most awkward looking design.

is that of the Swedish 64-gun ship *Wasa*, which sank on her maiden voyage in Stockholm harbour in 1628. Her sunken hull was discovered in 1956 and has been raised and is now being restored. A large number of carved figures, including a huge lion for the figurehead, were salvaged. For British ships, the work of the Dutch school of marine artists (especially the two Van de Veldes) is a useful source and of special importance was the new practice of building models of ships proposed for construction. Many ship-wrights were illiterate and plans of ships were very rare, so a scale model was a useful way of demonstrating the lines and features of an expensive new ship. Most of these 'Navy Board' models included exquisite miniature versions of the figurehead and all the other carvings. As carving and gilding on these late seventeenth-century ships cost a great deal, the administrators of the Royal Navy needed to see exactly what carved work they were paying for.

Like the *Sovereign of the Seas*, these warships were intended not just as fighting ships but as symbols of the power and prestige of their master, the king. The figurehead was the focus of a mass of carving that decorated the structural timbers of the beakhead and the bulkhead that ran across the ship behind them. The upper row of gunports was garlanded with carved and gilded laurel wreaths. The quarter galleries and the stern were a mass of carving, usually topped by the royal coat of arms. The most popular subject for the figurehead on warships of the late seventeenth and early eighteenth centuries was the crowned lion, symbolising power, speed and aggression. It became almost the standard figurehead for the smaller ships of the Royal Navy until 1750. A number of these lion figureheads have been preserved.

The great cost and weight of these decorations led to a gradual reduction in their scale, especially after 1700. The bow was treated with severely classical pilasters and architectural detail instead of human forms. The wreathed gunports gradually disappeared and the stern carvings were much reduced and made plainer and simpler in the same manner as the forward end of the ship. Yellow paint and eventually natural colours displaced costly gold leaf. This trend to scale down ornament continued for the rest of the era of fighting sailing ships but it did not

Many late eighteenth-century and early nineteenth-century warships were named after the heroes of ancient Greece and the figurehead of HMS 'Ajax' of 1809, now at the National Maritime Museum, is among the finest of these heroic carvings.

affect the figurehead for that above all was an expression of the personality of the ship and such emblems were important for the morale of the crew. Indeed figureheads were difficult to abolish even in the 1860s when the navy had turned to iron-hulled steamships.

The first-rate ships with a hundred or more guns — the most important in the fleet — were permitted elaborate figureheads even after the general restriction on ornament had been imposed. Large figures mounted on horseback were among the most popular and these were surrounded by coats of arms and figures representing military virtues.

By 1760 the carving of elaborate figureheads was on the wane. Falconer's *Marine Dictionary,* first published in 1769, commented: 'A multitude of ornaments appears rather unnecessary in any building calculated for the purpose of war. If there be any general rule to determine the subjects and quantity employed in shipbuilding, it seems to be connected with the ideas of dignity and simplicity . . . It is hardly possible for us to recollect the various disasters to which a single hero or goddess on the head of a ship is exposed by tempestuous weather, battle, and the unexpected encounter of ships, without trembling for the havoc and indecency that may happen to an assemblage of gods and conch shells, princesses and satyrs, heroes and blunderbusses, sea monsters, little children, globes and thunderbolts and all the apparatus necessary to constitute the head of a ship of the first class in our navy!'

The most popular figurehead was a single human form, sometimes full length, sometimes a bust of head and shoulders or three-quarter length. These usually had some connection with the name of the ship. The lion had waned in popularity and even the smaller warships carried individual designs. Many vessels carried the names of the heroes from Greek mythology.

The head was also gradually raised and made more compact. This made some of the full-length figures look very uncomfortable with their legs astride the stem and leaning back at the same time.

In 1796 the Royal Navy was ordered to

LEFT: *Governors, generals, kings and admirals were all represented in the figureheads of the early nineteenth-century battle fleet. This is a better example of a portrait than many. The figurehead of HMS 'Hastings', built at Calcutta in 1818, represents Lord Hastings, the governor general of India.*
RIGHT: *The Royal Navy economised on figurehead carving in the early nineteenth century. The figurehead of the 44-gun frigate HMS 'Isis' of 1819, preserved at HMS 'Camperdown', Royal Naval Reserve headquarters at Dundee, is a typical example of the simpler style of carving of this period.*

stop fitting figureheads to new ships and replace them with an abstract scroll or billethead. The order was not strictly observed for many seafarers felt that a ship without a figurehead would be an unlucky vessel. There was a decline in the standards of carving and many of the figureheads of the last wooden warships are crude by comparison with their predecessors. The development in the early nineteenth century of the round bow, which gave more strength to the forward end of the vessel and provided a better field of fire for the guns, greatly affected stem decoration. The figurehead became an isolated piece of ornament, with no elaborate trailboards or rails, and linked

to the ship by the broad yellow or white band which had become the standard painting practice for the navy.

The Royal Navy was very conservative in the early nineteenth century, preferring to retain the tried and trusted 'wooden walls' as the main battle fleet even into the 1850s, and with them their figureheads. They were so much part of the navy's tradition that they were placed even on the new iron steamers that were gradually being introduced in the 1860s.

Many nineteenth-century naval figureheads have been preserved. Many are crudely carved in comparison to earlier ones, especially in the anatomical detail on the human figureheads.

ABOVE LEFT: *The Royal Navy's first steam-powered warships carried figureheads. This example was carved for the iron paddle steamer HMS 'Caradoc', built at Blackwall in 1847.*
ABOVE RIGHT: *This gallant sailor from the sloop HMS 'Cruizer' of 1852 is interesting because he is a rating and neither a naval hero nor a figure in classical robes. Perhaps he was considered more appropriate for a small despatch vessel. He also wears the newly established uniform for the 'lower deck', the first ever for the ordinary sailors of the navy.*

BELOW: *Even after 'ironclad' warships had entirely superseded the 'wooden walls' figureheads were still fitted to some warships, such as this destroyer built by Lairds for the Chilean navy in the 1890s.*

ABOVE LEFT: *Figures in Highland dress were not uncommon. This female with targe and claymore belonged to the snow 'Caledonia', of Arbroath, wrecked at Morwenstow, Cornwall, in 1842, when on passage from Odessa to Gloucester with a cargo of wheat. The figurehead was erected in the churchyard as a memorial to her crew. She is a good example of the upright figure found on many early nineteenth-century ships.*

ABOVE RIGHT: *The carvers at small isolated shipyards sometimes produced lively and beautiful figureheads. This early Victorian lady with her bunch of grapes may have come from a West Country fruit schooner, one of the fastest of the small sailing ships. She is now at Southwold in Suffolk.*

LEFT: *By the mid nineteenth century an increasing number of figureheads were female, but few were as sensuous as this seductive Welsh lady.*

14

The British ports were crowded with hundreds of small wooden sailing ships and almost all of them carried a figurehead. This painting shows a typical scene, the Canada Dock, Liverpool, in the 1860s. Timber was often carried in old ships no longer fit for any other cargo. Here many bluff-bowed ships with the almost vertically positioned figureheads of the early nineteenth century can be seen.

FIGUREHEADS OF MERCHANT SHIPS

While figureheads on warships declined and disappeared during the nineteenth century, they flourished on merchant vessels. The British economy expanded during this period far more rapidly than ever before, under the impetus of the industrial revolution. Enormous quantities of goods were imported and exported from the British Isles and most were carried in British ships. British ships also dominated many of the other world trades for most of the nineteenth century and British shipbuilders took a major part in building ships for international trade. For over three quarters of this time goods were carried mainly in square-rigged sailing ships. Their numbers increased rapidly in the first half of the century but their design changed slowly. They were similar in size and rig to their predecessors of the seventeenth and eighteenth centuries and they were very small compared with later ships. For example the average size of vessel enter-ing the port of Liverpool in 1850 was under 500 tons.

The ships also kept the traditional decoration. Figureheads and stern carvings were considered an essential part of any new vessel and, as well as the sailing ships, many steamers carried figureheads until the straight bow became fashionable after 1870. At great ports like London, Glasgow and Liverpool astonishing fleets of vessels entered and left on every tide and more were tied up in the docks, displaying a marvellous range of wooden statuary.

The evidence for eighteenth-century merchant-ship figureheads is poor. An example of 1799 survives in the collection on board the preserved tea clipper *Cutty Sark* at Greenwich. But there are reliable paintings, and models and plans survive from the latter half of the century. The greatest of the merchant ships, those used by the East India Company for the Indian and Chinese trades, closely followed nav-

LEFT: *The public areas of naval shore bases are good places to see figureheads. There is a fine collection at HMS 'Nelson' at Portsmouth, including this massive harpist from the first-rate sailing warship HMS 'Hibernia' of 1804.*

RIGHT: *A finely carved figure in toga, tunic and sandals amidst the bowsprit rigging. Note the well executed scroll and leaf work on which he stands, and the figurehead of the iron ship 'Atlantic' in the background.*

al practice. Smaller vessels like the colliers delivering coal from the north-east of England to London had straight stems and no decoration, while others of similar size in other parts of the kingdom did. It seems that the more profitable the trade was the more likely a ship was to have a proper figurehead. Of the ships built by Brocklebanks at Whitehaven the larger vessels for the transatlantic trades seem to have been fitted with figureheads, while those destined largely for the Irish Sea trades only had billetheads. A rare model of a ship of 1750 shows a figurehead of a dragon-like beast while some of the ship portraits painted on punch bowls at Liverpool in the following decades show a preference for animals as figureheads. Towards the end of the century,

there is evidence for an increasing number of figureheads of people. This is to be found in the ship registers which were compiled for each port after 1786 and give a brief description of each ship's figurehead.

The bow shape of late eighteenth-century merchant ships gradually changed. As seen in the 1750 model the figure was in an upright position, but by about 1800 the whole of the head structure was lighter and the figure had been moved to a more forward leaning pose. The space between the head timbers was planked in and the head appeared much more of an integral part of the hull than before. This can be seen on the picture of the ships in Canada Dock, Liverpool.

In the mid nineteenth century a new

type of fast ship, the clipper, emerged. Clipper ships were of many varieties but all were intended to sail fast, even at the cost of reduced cargo capacity. The need for speedy ships with fine lines was stimulated by the requirement of quick deliveries in highly profitable trades such as that in China tea. A new design of bow evolved from this quest for speed. This was known as the *clipper bow*. In itself it was an expression of speed: the stem was sharply raking; the head above was extended forwards and lightened. The figurehead was at less of an angle and there was a greater emphasis on decorating the supporting timbers, the trailboards, behind the figurehead. This had the pleasing effect of harmonising the line of the figurehead with the upward curve of the hull — the sheer of the ship. These features are well illustrated by R. R. Laurie's design for a clipper ship of the 1860s.

Figureheads for British eighteenth-century merchantmen are rare. This little beast on the bows of a contemporary model of a ship of about 1750 is therefore an extremely interesting survival.

The most important change of the nineteenth century was the development of reliable ocean-going steamers. Regular transatlantic steamer services were well established by 1850 and thereafter steamers took a gradually increasing share of the regular and more profitable trades, but the sailing ship, with its lower operating costs, continued to carry most of the lower paying freights such as coal and grain until the 1890s. The early steamers, whether paddle or screw, normally carried a full set of sails to economise on coal and in case the engines broke down. They retained the traditional bow layout including a figurehead. Straight stems for steamers became the norm by the 1870s and the fitting of figureheads ended. However, a few passenger liners and steam yachts were built with clipper bows and figureheads to enhance their appearance.

J. J. Laurie's design is typical of the clipper ship era. Note the elaborate design of the trailboards and the way they merge into the figurehead.

ABOVE LEFT: *The craftsmen who carved the figureheads are usually anonymous. This is a rare self-portrait bust by William Dodd, one of the Liverpool shipcarvers, who was at work from the 1850s until about 1900.*

ABOVE RIGHT: *The designs of the Liverpool carver R. Lee display some of the great variety of mid nineteenth-century figureheads.*

BELOW: *Another carver who is known was A. E. Anderson of Bristol. His trade sign incorporates scrollwork of the kind typically used for trailboards. Some of his tools are on display at Madame Tussaud's, Wookey Hole, Somerset.*

ABOVE: *Some figureheads were modelled from life, perhaps from a member of the shipowner's family. This stern lady was designed by William Dodd for the ship 'Denmark'. He must have drawn her from life for she is no beauty!*

LEFT: *This cheerful Jack Tar was once a tobacconist's sign. He reminds us that many shipcarvers also worked on carvings for shops, pubs and houses in seaport towns.*

Sailing ships also changed. After 1860 more of the deep-sea ships were built of iron or steel, although small coastal ships continued to be built of wood. Much larger vessels could be built of iron than of wood and the sailing ships of the second half of the nineteenth century had in many cases double or treble the cargo space of their predecessors. They were increasingly concentrated on carrying bulk cargoes. These giant sailing ships continued the tradition of ship decoration but in a simplified form. The elaborate trailboards behind the figurehead gradually shrank in size until the figurehead was left by itself. This can be seen on the *Celtic Glen.*

The subjects for figureheads were many and various. The deep-sea vessels tended to have human figures and at the beginning of the nineteenth century male and female figureheads were equally popular, but by the 1880s female figureheads easily predominated. Abstract designs such as billetheads and coats of arms were also frequent on the later ships. They were presumably an economy measure. There were many other designs as well. This is demonstrated by the work of the Liverpool shipcarver R. Lee, though whether he carved all the designs himself is uncertain. Also popular were warriors and statesmen as well as characters in popular literature. The works of Sir Walter Scott and Robert Burns inspired the naming and therefore the figureheads of many Scottish built or owned ships, including the *Cutty Sark*, whose figurehead is derived from Burns's poem 'Tam o' Shanter'. Relatives and friends of the shipowner or the owner himself were common subjects; for example, John Gambles, a Cumbrian shipowner, had two ships built and named after himself and his wife, Anne, and each carried a figurehead portrait of its namesake. James Baines, owner of the Black Ball Line, sat for his figurehead portrait at the Liverpool workshop of Allan and Clotworthy and when finished it was sent to Boston to be fitted on his large new clipper, the *James Baines.* Many of the less beautiful lady figureheads, where there is no personal name or the identity of the ship was not known, were probably carved as portraits of wives or daughters.

ABOVE: *John Gambles, a shipowner of the Cumbrian port of Maryport, in 1874 added to his fleet a ship which he named after himself. Its figurehead is his carved portrait.*

BELOW: *The rusty ship 'Celtic Glen' has a fine lady in druidic dress at the bows, but as with many of the last big sailing ships there are no supporting ornamental trailboards.*

ABOVE: *Although most steamships were built with straight stems and no figureheads after the 1860s, passenger liners were occasionally built with clipper bows and figureheads, with pleasing results. This ship is Canadian Pacific's 'Empress of Japan' of 1891.*

LEFT: *The figurehead tended to reflect the name of the ship. Even politicians had ships named after them and the schooner 'C. S. Parnell' had a bust of the great Irish leader.*

BELOW: *The small sailing ships in the coastal trades could not always afford the expense of a properly carved figurehead. This seagull from the wooden ketch 'Bessie Clark', built at Bideford in 1881, was possibly the work of one of the crew, carved some time after the launch of the vessel.*

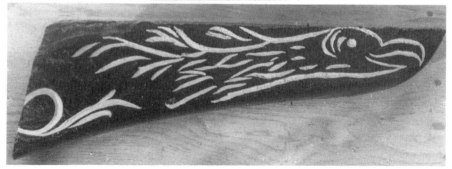

Many of the early steamships carried figureheads. It was only with the progress in iron hulls in the 1860s that the figurehead began to be omitted. This fine example came from the pioneer paddle steamer 'Sirius', one of the first vessels to cross the Atlantic under power, and is on display at the Town Docks Museum, Hull.

Animals and birds were other sources of inspiration. The early transatlantic steamer *Sirius* had a splendid dog, representing the Dog Star, and Corsar Line ships carried the figure of the flying horse Pegasus. In most cases the figurehead was designed to reflect the name of the vessel but towards the end of the century there seems to have been an increase in fairly standard lady figureheads which often had no connection with the vessel's name. One of the most unusual figureheads carved at this time was that of the ship *Bates Family,* which reverted to the group figurehead type of the eighteenth century with seven members of the shipowner's family represented on the bow. Unfortunately no picture of this unique carving has survived.

Ships were built in nearly every port, however big or small, around the coasts of the British Isles in the nineteenth century and usually the figurehead was carved at the same place. In the bigger ports there were specialised workshops which carved figureheads and ship decorations to the order of the shipyards. The Glasgow carvers J. and R. R. Laurie, for example, supplied work to many of the Clydeside yards as well as exporting figureheads to Canada between about 1850 and 1870. But little is known about individual carvers. They are seldom mentioned in reports of new ships. Brooker of Maryport, who carved for the *John Gambles,* had quite a local reputation. William Dodd of Liverpool, who carved the *James Baines* figurehead, is known because he carved a self portrait and one of his sketchbooks has survived. A. E. Anderson is recognised because his huge trade sign has survived and others are known, like A. P. Elder of Glasgow, whose sketchbook is at the National Maritime Museum. Most of these craftsmen seem to have had difficulty in finding enough work on figureheads alone. Anderson is known to have carved roundabout horses and the two Lauries carved religious figures for a church, a

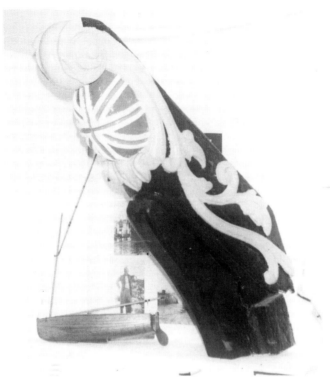

LEFT: *Patriotic emblems were always popular. This is the head of the schooner (later ketch) 'Emma Louise' of 1883, which incorporates the Union Jack into the design. It is on show at the North Devon Maritime Museum, Appledore.*

BELOW: *The work on abstract bow decorations could be just as pleasing as the figurehead in human form. This is the head of the topsail schooner 'Kathleen and May' preserved by the Maritime Trust at St Katharine's Dock, London.*

ABOVE: *All over the world seafaring communities have decorated their craft with figureheads. This is a striking example from a Maori war canoe. The figure has its tongue stuck out in defiance of the enemy.*

RIGHT: *The four-masted barque 'Falkirk' was one of the last deep-sea commercial sailing ships to be built. Her figurehead survived for some years after the ship was scrapped and had a well carved head with rather crude neck and draperies.*

The famous emigrant ship 'Marco Polo' had a standing figurehead which was typical of both naval and merchant ships of the early nineteenth century.

sign for the office of a friendly society and much else. Even today in seaports there are shops and pubs of the Victorian era with abstract carved decoration which is reminiscent of the designs for trailboards and other ship carving.

It is not known how the carvers were trained. Apprenticeship is likely but R. R. Laurie may have attended classes at the Glasgow School of Art and Design. The sketchbook seems to have been the main method of working out the design. Occasionally there was a model, like the 1765 design for HMS *Victory,* but this method does not seem to have been used for merchant ships nor do any full-size plans seem to have been employed. The tools of the shipcarver, judging from the few of Anderson's that have been preserved, were the same as any other carver's, and the timber used seems to have varied, though Canadian yellow pine was favoured in the nineteenth century. Many of the larger figureheads were made from several pieces of timber and these were often fastened together by copper bolts.

Although they were never as highly decorated as naval vessels, merchant ships usually had more than just the figurehead, at least until the 1880s. Much of this work, such as the trailboards, cabin skylights and the carving on the stern, would usually consist of abstract patterns: scrolls, acanthus leaves, strapwork and so on. In the nineteenth century much of this work seems to have been similar to other kinds of patterned decoration ashore. Both may have been inspired by the books of ornament and design which were popular at the time. Occasionally stern carvings were more elaborate than the normal ornamental frame for the ship's name and port of registry, but this seems to have been a North American tradition.

ABOVE: *Many ships built in North America for British shipowners had interesting stern carvings. This is one of a pair of carvings from the stern of the record-breaking emigrant clipper 'Marco Polo' showing the famous Venetian explorer in oriental and nineteenth-century western dress.*

BELOW: *This splendid elephant also came from the stern decoration of the 'Marco Polo'.*

ABOVE LEFT: *Figureheads are still to be found in places other than museums. This is the famous early eighteenth-century lion at the Red Lion inn at Martlesham, Suffolk.*

ABOVE RIGHT: *Many fine foreign figureheads are to be found in British museums. This one came from the French warship 'Franklin' of 1787, which was captured at the battle of the Nile and renamed HMS 'Canopus'.*

RIGHT: *The fate of many figureheads, after their ship had gone, was to be hung up on the outside of a building and then forgotten. The figurehead of the schooner 'Rosebud' was in danger of splitting in two when she was rescued. Unfortunately many other fine examples, which survived all the perils of the sea, have since been lost through neglect.*

The art of figurehead carving never disappeared completely. This example was carved for the training ship HMS 'Conway' in 1938 by Carter Preston, who also carved stone gargoyles for Liverpool cathedral. It can now be seen at the Portsmouth shore station (left). The right-hand picture shows it in position on the bows of the 'Conway'.

FIGUREHEADS TODAY

All but a few sailing ships have long since disappeared, through either shipwreck or the breaker's yard, but many of their figureheads have survived, taken as trophies from wrecks and even used as memorials in churchyards to the crew who were drowned. Many were hung up in shipyards and the streets of seaports as cheerful decorations. Unfortunately, many of those that were put up in the open have since rotted away from neglect. The figurehead of the *Falkirk*, which survived in the Rock Ferry tea gardens at Birkenhead until the Second World War, has vanished and that of the *Rosebud*, which graced a builder's yard, had split almost in two by the time it was rescued. Moreover, many of the surviving figureheads have lost their names through being parted from their ships.

The named ones, however, often have stories linked to them: for example, the figurehead of the ship *Lottie Sleigh* was preserved as a reminder of a legal case important in insurance history after the ship blew up with a cargo of gunpowder in 1864; and the figurehead of the Spanish barque *Primos,* wrecked on the Scillies in 1871, was used by the sole survivor as a liferaft. A number of naval figureheads came from ships captured by the Royal Navy in the eighteenth century and put into service as Royal Navy ships. These include the eighty-gun French ship *Franklin* of 1787, with its fine martial figurehead, captured by Nelson's fleet at the Battle of the Nile. She was accepted into the Royal Navy as HMS *Canopus.*

Figureheads occasionally appear for sale in antique shops and auctions and they are still to be found in public places. What is thought to be the oldest surviving figurehead is still serving as an inn sign at the Red Lion, Martlesham in Suffolk.

LEFT: *The majestic figurehead of the iron ship 'Allahabad' of 1864 is a good example of the shipcarver's art. Note the carving of her draperies.*
RIGHT: *The pious figurehead of the schooner 'Beatrice' was rescued from her rotting hulk at Widnes, Cheshire, in the 1950s. Though the carving is not particularly fine, her facial expression has been rendered with great feeling.*

Many naval figureheads are still treasured by the Royal Navy. The training establishments that were once housed in old wooden warships retained their figureheads after the ships were scrapped. The great naval bases of Devonport, Chatham and Portsmouth and the former naval depot at Sheerness all have interesting collections but these are not always accessible to the general visitor. The best public collection is at the Royal Naval Museum, which is attached to HMS *Victory* at Portsmouth. Here there are thirty-seven figureheads, all from warships, and ranging from the *Warrior* of 1781 to the *Espiegle* of 1900, one of the last warships ever to be fitted with a figurehead.

The National Maritime Museum at Greenwich has a large collection which is predominantly naval and includes some good examples of lion figureheads, many fine late eighteenth-century pieces such as HMS *Ajax* and HMS *Canopus* and examples of the cruder nineteenth-century naval carvings. The largest collection of figureheads from merchant ships is also in Greenwich, on board the preserved tea clipper *Cutty Sark*. There are over one hundred pieces of carving and they were collected by John Cumbers (Long John Silver) of Gravesend in the 1920s and 1930s and presented to the *Cutty Sark* in 1957.

Most coastal museums have at least one figurehead. The Town Docks Museum, Hull, has a good collection, including the dog from the steamer *Sirius,* and there is a growing collection at Merseyside Maritime Museum, Liverpool. The Valhalla Maritime Museum on the island of Tresco in the Scillies has one of the finest collections of ship carvings in the world. It was founded by Augustus Smith, Lord Proprietor of the Scilly Isles, in about 1840 and represents what has been saved from more than one thousand wrecks in the past two centuries.

Other types of figurehead can also be seen in museums. Seafaring societies beyond Europe also decorated their craft. For example, among the hundreds of scattered islands in the Pacific the small tribal groups developed their own

Figurehead carving revived. Mr J. Whitehead and Mr N. Gaches at work on their figurehead for the restored HMS 'Warrior' which is on display at Portsmouth.

craft with individual decorations. Many of them had a religious significance, reflecting the importance of ships to these islanders for communication and survival. There are many examples of their figurehead carving art in British museums. Among the most spectacular are those carved by the Maoris of New Zealand, which incorporate both figures, usually monster-like and defiant, and superbly intricate interlaced carving.

The ships of today have little or no decoration, let alone a figurehead. Nonetheless there are occasional reminders: for example, many ships still have their owner's badge or logo painted on their bows or sterns. A pleasing British example is the 'Legs of Man' badge carried by the ships of the Isle of Man Steam Packet Company. But figurehead carving has never completely died out. Most of the sail training ships that have been built in the twentieth century have carried them. A good traditional one was carved in 1938 for the old wooden warship HMS *Conway*, which was a stationary school ship. By contrast the four-masted schooner *Albatross*, built for training Swedish cadets after the Second World War and now no longer a sailing ship, had a striking and new interpretation of the figurehead: the graceful silhouette of an albatross in flight on either side of the bow.

The art of figurehead carving has undergone a small revival since the early 1960s. This has been linked with the movement to restore and preserve full-size ships, especially sailing ships, and mostly in the United States. Mystic Seaport Museum has a figurehead carver's workshop where work is carried on in front of visitors, but some of the best of the new figureheads have been carved by British craftsmen such as Jack Whitehead and Norman Gaches of the Isle of Wight and Trevor Ellis of Emsworth, Hampshire. Jack Whitehead, besides restoring many old figures, has also carved new ones, like that of the four-masted ship *Falls of Clyde* preserved in Hawaii and that for HMS *Warrior* of 1859.

FURTHER READING

Carr Laughton, L. G. *Old Ship Figure-Heads and Sterns*. 1925. Classic and now rare book principally about naval decorations.

Frere-Cook, G. (editor). *The Decorative Arts of the Mariner*. 1966.

Hansen, Hans Jurgen. *Galionsfiguren*. West Germany, 1979. A worldwide catalogue of most figureheads in museums, superbly illustrated; text in German, but not difficult to follow.

Norton, Peter. *Ships' Figureheads*. 1976. A helpful, wide-ranging survey with many illustrations.

Randier, Jean. *Nautical Antiques for the Collector*. 1976. Some good illustrations.

PLACES TO VISIT

Cutty Sark Clipper Ship, King William Walk, Greenwich, London SE10 9BG. Telephone: 081-858 3445.

Merseyside Maritime Museum, Albert Dock, Pier Head, Liverpool L3 1DN. Telephone: 051-709 1551.

Museum of Transport, Kelvin Hall, 1 Bunhouse Road, Glasgow G3 8DP. Telephone: 041-357 3929.

The National Maritime Museum, Romney Road, Greenwich, London SE10 9NF. Telephone: 081-858 4422.

Royal Naval Museum, HM Naval Base, Portsmouth, Hampshire PO1 3LR. Telephone: (0705) 733060. HMS *Victory* and HMS *Warrior* are berthed here.

Town Docks Museum, Queen Victoria Square, Hull HU1 3DX. Telephone: (0482) 222737/8.

Valhalla Museum, Tresco Abbey, Tresco, Isles of Scilly. Telephone: (0720) 22849.